D1280228

Fragment of the Head of a Queen

Fragment of the Head of a Queen
poems by Cate Marvin

Sarabande  Books
LOUISVILLE, KENTUCKY

Managing Editor
Sarabande Books, Inc.
2234 Dundee Road, Suite 200
Louisville, KY 40205

Library of Congress Cataloging-in-Publication Data

Marvin, Cate, 1969–
    Fragment of the head of a queen : poems / by Cate Marvin. — 1st ed.
        p.   cm.
    ISBN-13: 978-1-932511-51-2 (pbk. : alk. paper)
    ISBN-10: 1-932511-51-2 (pbk. : alk. paper)
    I. Title.

    PS3563.A74294F73 2007
    811'.6—dc22   2006032135

ISBN-13: 978-1-932511-51-2

Cover image: *Study for When Alone Again*/Hammer Museum, 2001, by Arturo Herrera. Colored pencil on paper, 52 x 48 inches. Image courtesy of Sikkema Jenkins & Co.

Cover and text design by Charles Casey Martin

Manufactured in Canada
This book is printed on acid-free paper.

Sarabande Books is a nonprofit literary organization.

This project is supported in part by an award from the National Endowment for the Arts.

The Kentucky Arts Council, a state agency in the Commerce Cabinet, provides operational support funding for Sarabande Books with state tax dollars and federal funding from the National Endowment for the Arts, which believes that a great nation deserves great art.

for boys and their mothers

Contents

Part II

Acknowledgments

Many thanks to the editors of the journals in which the following poems first appeared, sometimes in different versions:

Alaska Quarterly: "Cloud Elegy"
American Literary Review: "Lines for a Mentor"
Boston Review: "Coup de Soleil"
The Canary: "Love the Contagion"; "Pan"
The Cincinnati Review: "Orange Drink Man"
Columbia: A Journal for Literature and the Arts: "Catatonia"
Columbia Poetry Review: "Pretty Speech (The Occasion of Your
        Death"; "Colder, Bitterer"; "You Cut Open"
Conundrum Engine Literary Review: "A Brief Attachment"
CutBank: "Mug Shot"; "Mushrooms"
Fence: "After the Last Fright"
The Kenyon Review: "Scenes from the Battle of Us"; "Azaleas"
Mid-American Review: "She Wishes Her Beloved Were Dead";
        "Teens Love Horse Dick"
New England Review: "A Windmill Makes a Statement";
        "My Black Address"; "Lying My Head Off"
Ninth Letter: "A Fainting Couch"; "Flowers, Always"; "Landscape
        with Hungry Girls"; "'Practically an Oprhan'"
Ploughshares: "Robotripping"; "Monsterful"
Poetry: "Fragment of the Head of a Queen"; "Muckraker"
POOL: "NyQuil"
Provincetown Arts: "Your Call Is Very Important to Us"
Slate: "The Pet"; "Postscript"; "The Unfortunates"
Tin House: "All My Wives"; "Your Childhood"
TriQuarterly: "Little Poem That Tries"; "Poem That Wears
        Your Scarf"

Verse: "Stone Fruit"
Washington Square: "Alibi Poem"; "Flood Museum"

The Sappho epigraph is taken from Guy Davenport's translation: *Archilichus, Sappho, Alkman: Three Lyric Poets of the Late Greek Bronze Age.* Berkeley: University of California Press, 1980.

For friendship and editorial insight, I wish to thank: Rick Barot, Joshua Beckman, Don Bogen, Nickole Brown, Steven Cramer, Jim Cummins, Amber Dermont, Michael Dumanis, John Drury, Josh Edwards, Thomas Sayers Ellis, Monica Ferrell, Kirby Gann, Sarah Gorham, Ed Hirsch, Kevin Honold, Rodney Jones, Larry Joseph, LW#1, Fred Kaufman, the Marvin family, Maureen McLane, Sarah Messer, ZZ Packer, Lee Papa, Blanford Parker, Robert Pinksy, Paisley Rekdal, Robyn Schiff, Jeffrey Skinner, Christina Tortora, Nick Twemlow, and Matt Yeager. Thanks also to my colleagues and students at the Lesley University Low-Residency M.F.A. Program in Creative Writing and the College of Staten Island, City University of New York. Many thanks to Zav and Linda Giragosian for allowing me to work in their lovely home during the final stages of writing this book.

I am grateful to Arturo Herrera for kindly allowing me to use his painting "Study for When Alone Again, 2001" as the cover art for this book. Likewise, I am thankful to Jeff Smith for first introducing me to Herrera's work and to Jeewon Jung for her artistic insight.

The completion of this book was greatly aided by the generosity of the University of Cincinnati's Department of English, Claremont Graduate University, Bread Loaf Writers' Conference, Sewanee Writers' Conference, the Academy of American Poets, the Virginia Center for Creative Arts, the College of Staten Island, the Professional Staff Congress of the City University of New York, and the Corporation of Yaddo.

In Memoriam: Drew Wilson (1980–2005)

And who shall tell the amorist
Oblivion is so loverless.

—Dylan Thomas

Don't stir
The trash.

—Sappho

Fragment of the Head of a Queen

Part I

Love the Contagion

Quest the contagion, funnel much muck
through your hands upraised and cupped,
pour river-brack down your throat, pick
your scabs with loving glee. Love your

master of pestilence, conqueror of white
clothes: mud prints, paw prints, germs
not even the physician knows. Eat through
a muskrat's lair, divine the grub's slumber

beneath rotting leaves, take the lot, crush
it in your bare hands. Look at the moon
for its holes, narrow your eye at its skin
until you find its pores, squint your eyes

at the filthy sun and run toward the flavor
factory where the cherry stench hangs
above the highway, the machines that cast
that bright net of scent into the polluted air:

its mix of chemical so thick your breath
trips as if you're inhaling jello. Lap at its
stickiness, run your rough hands through
your own gnarled hair. Repel the lover,

cast his grace at broken ground. Wear
your lover's indiscretions like stickpins

in your apple hat: rotting skin, dry as dust,
ample-sliced, a great old pie atop your head!

Be the world. Do not deny our fascination
lies in its filth, the maggot's sweet diet.
Marvel at the corrupt! Make disgust your
lust and cast your fresh pain to the trash!

The Pet

I rode him through the village, smiling.
He tossed his tasseled mane in distress.
The villagers took his gesture as vanity,
and made no attempt to rein him back.
Camped at night by stream and fire,

he seemed to think stories were in order.
The ghoulish tales twisting out his mouth
no longer frightened me. On leaving,
I'd taken on a certain complacency. Later,
he'd characterize my silence as merely

mean. But what is mean about a mouth
that, having no stories, claims it can provide
no flower for the ear, no wine for the wind?
I tried: I told the tale of him, which he
(the version being mine) was not much

interested in. But all of us, the fattening
moon, the yewey trees, the sharp-toothed
stars who combed their glowing backs against
the sky like cats: we laughed. And now
that I had left, where would I take him?

He was vehicle and, as such, responsibility.
He was deadening, tiresome, and necessary.
I made ourselves a home and kept him gently

as a pet. Visitors often wonder aloud,
How do you manage to keep such a creature

inside? The floors are stained with his keep.
I tell them my heart is huge and its doors
are small. Once I took him in he grew. Now
I cannot remove him without killing him,
which, frankly, I have never wanted to do.

Azaleas

It was a town so quiet, the mailman was empty-handed.
Why then nostrils of bloom, breathing so pinkly?

Even the town crier had taken a vow of silence.
Why at the house's edge, beneath a wide-eyed window?

A pink so dense it begged hiding. Unsiblinged, unmated,
the moon might find one rocking in a hedge of pink.

It was a town clothed from head to toe: skirts draped
its ankles, sleeves were buttoned tight at its wrists.

So why a shimmered curtain, less a curtain than a sheer
view of two figures on a bed, eyes affixed to a blue flickering?

Blooms pink as baby mice, soft as tiny hands, cluttering
the bush as if in celebration. Why a town that never smiled?

A figure lifted an arm to the nightstand, drank long a glass
of amber. Blue light flickered to the metronome of drama.

Nobody touched nobody. Invisible figures mowed lawns
soundlessly. The halls, everywhere, blue and institutional.

Where cars never drove with their windows rolled down.
A town where anything might happen, except for me.

The flowers, only the flowers had hearts. Even birds
pretended, their beating of wings mechanized by meanness.

Except for the petals that touched my fingers, except
for the little oceans I viewed their pinks through,

except the tongue that was my nose, the whiskers
I wore as I crawled on my knees through yards,

beneath the fresh fingers of azalea blooms, beneath
a window that flickered blue, to where my smile grew.

She Wishes Her Beloved Were Dead

It punches like liquor to the gut. And it is enough.
How you swerve into the parking lot. And I only want
to get you drunk enough. I want your stare like a shot.
The Lamplighter's open till 2. That's late enough.

I think we've done well for ourselves. On the porch,
tongues sharp with Scotch. Outside the squat house
you've rented, we shine like crystals in the desert.
The moon is cast in a sky waylaid by ash. The one lit

bedside lamp flickers from inside with the shadows
of flies. It's only 3, so I tip the bottle toward your glass.
Brash, my hand remembers its place on your knee.
But you're as prim as a closed umbrella, useless in this

arid climate. You sniff as if you can smell a wedding
in the air, as if your parasol opens only for rain.
Dear less-than-a-man, I think with my blood.
The tufted blossoms of the Mimosa tree are pink,

but the female of the species is known to stink.
Stifling a yawn, you sink further back into your chair.
You say you hope we'll have a chance to rendezvous
some other time. No mention is made of where.

When you breathe deep in sleep, I hang from the rafters
like a bat. Dreaming of mother-hate, your limbs twitch

beneath the sheets. All night I swing above you, still drunk from sipping at your chest: pale, tiny teacups.

After the Last Fright

I carved upon my desk unsayables.
He drank until he vomited on himself.
Eavesdropping, the others resisted sleep.
The house knew the pain of sun on lacquered floorboards.

I carved it with the tips of scissors.
A door creaked; he hung his head into the room.
Please, the others cannot sleep.
The shingles twitched like skin beneath moonlight.

I spent the afternoon at a movie theater.
He staggered through brush toward a pay phone.
The others continued searching the streets for him.
The house held the moon above it, it was that imperial.

I recall the room was empty when I came back in.
He was arrested at the Quik-Trip while calling collect.
Frantic, the others circled the block again.
The house was ghost-white, older than the dead.

I needle-pointed for 72 hours straight.
He claimed the whole situation humiliated him.
Relieved, the others refrained from asking him what jail was like.
The house was swan to field, tiger to sea.

I lay in bed by the time the others came home.
He couldn't recall putting on the orange jumpsuit.

The others asked if I'd seen him around.
The house shuddered, *No-o-o-o.*

The house winced, winked its blinds.
The house whispered I should stay inside.
The others flew out the doors and into their cars.
The others slammed their cars into deer and cried.

He was more humiliated than he'd ever been.
He looked more or less the same, though his eyes were ringed.
The others hid in the basement.
He climbed the stairs and presented a ring.

The house swung its windows wide to ice.
He banged his nails blue, pinned his tongue to his tie.
He packed himself in a box, sent it to regions far off.
The others pressed their ears to the pipes.

The house wore its flames like a hat.
The house called a radio talk-show.
We drank all night, laughed all night, the night he left.
I shook in its mouth till the house drank me up.

Lines for a Mentor

I am driving a screw into the plump of a cork.
I am ignoring the animal tracks left on my face.
I am lying at the bottom of a clothes hamper.

Bees crowd a trash can: a bouquet of stings.
I once asked a teacher where a letter begins.
How prickly I felt as I sat within his walls:

peach-hued, smoothly painted with Zen patience.
If I am to take his advice, I'll start with where
I am presently. I am a pelt full of gunshot,

too torn in death to be made a coat. I've endured
an eclipse each day, have learned to train my eyes
to avoid the sky's direct gaze. I take the sun's light

and put it on bread, eat daily a sandwich of red.
I never wanted to build a house without nails,
I never wanted to bend a horseshoe's glowing iron.

Or desired to landscape a garden where rare buttery
moths would arrive each night for nectar. I won't lie
and say I didn't mind, that I didn't cry once,

wanting to make the teacher mine, so I might
be him. He said, *Never strike a typewriter,*
for they are delicate instruments. I am crouched

beneath the threat of toppling bookshelves.

Of all the change that rattles in my head, the pennies

are his: not worth much, yet not entirely worthless.

Cloud Elegy

The world felt bad. Every leaf looked
like it needed a cigarette. Gutters took
cups strewn at their lips, turned them
upright to offer tiny pleas for change.
Windows enacted a communal decision
to condense, despite the consistent lack
of rain. All lungéd things grew asthmatic,
did not know whether it was the smog
or sheer anxiety rendering them unable
to breathe. Doves, those trusted symbols
of fidelity, engaged in the most tawdry
affairs, could not have told you where
their hearts lay, even if you could have
pointed them out, say, in that ditch over
there. And although the sex was great,
being both untoward and ill-conceived,
the world was relieved to get a prescription.
The clouds became patients and allowed
their numb griefs to occlude our skyline.
Streets suddenly looked so tame, so placid
outside the bleary windows. And with just
a pill, millions of pills, the world didn't
mind how awfully anxious and American
things had gotten. So what if our lives
were rotten? We were ready, anesthetized,

to face another century, the clouds a little
less gossamer, a little less reminiscent
of the shapes we had wished to take.

Pan

And if I loved a man with fawn-hued
trousers and shoes cleft, with new nubs
      just apparent on his just-shaved head,
I might learn how to find the udder of
      the sky, suck its blue-milk, be less than
taken aback by its startling color.

      Should he heft me over his shoulder,
place me down by the edge of a frozen river,
wash my hair in twig-tangled ice, put his
      mouth hot at my ear, speak shell-
soft, I think I might allow him to melt
      me before an indoor fire, leave me

ragged, thaw me out with his unruly stare.
      Perhaps then, he'll offer a book from
his tongue, his journeys through Siberia, his
      nights quiet beneath tents in Senegal.
I'll know of the wine-dyed lips his mouth has
lipped. He'll speak soft of undulating bodies.

      I'll hear it without jealousy. The book,
embroidered with dust, will fall from his
satchel, read itself to me. That afternoon
      we'll lie beneath the Chynna tree,
      breathe its softly graying shadow,
and I will let his tongue move across my teeth.

In three days hence, I will leave, don this metal
shield, saddle my volatile horse, part knowing
          he will always breathe beneath the spring
of my absence. Or perhaps I will walk him into
          the smoke-filled eye of the Bear Cat lounge,
          where we'll sit on barstools, exchange

hands. His hand is rough, yet his nails shine
          with moons. His teeth are strong: canine.
          Our hands are doing the talking—but
before the door is knocked by that other fist (which
          I must admit as love)—there is so much
I want to say. So I say *Seas*, I say *Distance*.

A Windmill Makes a Statement

You think I like to stand all day, all night,
all any kind of light, to be subject only
to wind? You are right. If seasons undo
me, you are my season. And you are the light
making off with its reflection as my stainless
steel fins spin.

               On lawns, on lawns we stand,
we windmills make a statement. We turn air,
churn air, turning always on waiting for your
season. There is no lover more lover than the air.
You care, you care as you twist my arms
round, till my songs become popsicle

and I wing out radiants of light all across
suburban lawns. You are right, the churning
is for you, for you are right, no one but you
I spin for all night, all day, restless for your

sight to pass across the lawn, tease grasses,
because I so like how you lay above me,
how I hovered beneath you, and we learned
some other way to say: *There you are.*

*You strip the cut, splice it to strips, you mill
the wind, you scissor the air into ecstasy until
all lawns shimmer with your bluest energy.*

19

Scenes from the Battle of Us

You are like a war novel, entirely lacking
female characters, except for an occasional
letter that makes one of the men cry.

> I am like a table
> that eats its own legs off
> because it's fallen
> in love with the floor.

My frantic hand can't find where my leg
went. You can play the tourniquet. A tree
with white limbs will grow here someday.

> Or maybe a pup tent
> that's collapsed in on itself,
> it so loves the sleep
> of men sleeping beneath it.

The reason why women dislike war movies
may have something to do with why men hate
romantic comedies: they are both about war.

> Perhaps I should
> live in a pig's trough.
> There, I'd be wanted.
> There, I'd be tasted.

When the mailbag drops from the sky
and lands heavy on the jungle floor, its letters
are prepared to swim away with your tears.

One letter reads:
I can barely feel
furtive. The other:
I am diminishing.

Gaslight

He asked to split a ream of paper
so I foolishly handed him the whole
sheaf, reminding him I'd be wanting
its other half back. Now I'm typing
on the ink-soaked ends of old papers,
squinting my eyes so as not to see
through their skins, read backwards
yesterday's or last month's intentions.

The same happened to my envelopes,
and let's not forget the paper clips,
and I used to have a full box of pens.
Now, they turn up beneath the sofa,
ends bitten as if the dogs were nervous,
or he (frown a crumpled napkin across
his brow) chomped an afternoon away.
I'm surprised to find my hands still

attached to the ends of my arms, which
I keep fastened to my sides as I pretend
to sleep, tongue locked behind my teeth,
words hoarded into that little corral that
sits in the furthest corner of my mind.
Sometimes, I think he's got into the wine,
spilled a little down the sink to make me
think I'm drinking more than I used to.

When I knock at his door to ask back
for my calculator, his look knocks me
down, his door slams me out. When my
tailbone hits the floor and I cry out, he
applauds me for being *such a fine actress!*
Let us see how he takes my absence. I am
packing up my desk. And I'll let him keep
the scissors. He'll find them in his back.

My Black Address

Forward me no more the mail sent
to that old address. No roses were

ever delivered to that door. My head
still sits stuck atop a spear and sings

the cannibal's song from the back
porch. A sort of lullaby for neighbors

who miss us. And, O, the flowers
still grow, more lushly than before,

the raw blooms fed at their root's
very foot by the marrow from my

discarded bones. Hands are shards
picked at by birds, and my skull's

become a cemetery for the mice.
And the red rat, with its mottled tail,

still survives in the crumbling shed
with its roof rusting apart. And still

he gnaws at the lilacs. How did we
learn that the nearby zoo once flushed

droves of rats out, that they entered
into the cellars of that neighborhood

as poison drives into the blood, as
disease thrives in the veins of the ill?

In the worst days, he blamed me for
the fact the last he saw of his father's

face was in an open casket. But it is
not true that he looked at all. I looked

while he looked away. I wanted to see
what the terrible man looked like, and

then he only looked like a man, and
a dead one at that. I think my hands

are buried out back, deep, where
honeysuckle twists and, the neighbors

said, there used to be a goldfish pond,
which was why the earth was so damp

down that little slope. I do not recall
what it was to kiss him. I haven't been

able to look at the moon the same since.
It feels as if it bit me. I remember how he

used to stand me over the heating vent
and that he would kiss, but not the kiss.

I did not know that I'd love memory
more for its mercy and less for the damp

visitations of his flashing change, twisting
mouth an aorta of grief. I have changed

my address, but it is no less black. It is
a lake's surface plated with onyx. You

can see yourself among the glaring numerals.
Your face will not grow wider with terror,

for it cannot go any wider with terror,
and there is, at last, small comfort in that.

Teens Love Horse Dick

So much pornography one cannot afford.
They say there's a lady who spreads herself
so wide she welcomes inside the entire world.
So many innuendos I would prefer to miss.
A man said all young girls who love horses
are naturally suspect. He raised an eyebrow.

When he left, all he left was trash. A closet
clogged with old shirts and letters, note cards
on which he'd listed things he'd wished I had
done for him naked, but hadn't. When young,
there was nothing I wanted more than a horse.
On the cards, his cursive soared toward what

he'd wanted. There was no room for a horse
in the city where I grew, so I began collecting
plastic models. I had a tiny leather saddle for
my favorite. What it was he needed, I must
have managed to ignore. After we split our
address, I read his notes, acquired this injury.

My questions are numerous: How did they get
my address? If teens do, in actuality, love
horse dick, how did I remain unaware of this
preoccupation throughout my adolescence?
They say they take credit cards. They say
we should drive down the coast and cross

over into Mexico, they suggest we head first
to see a donkey show, where a lady spreads
herself so wide you can see constellations beam
out from inside of her. This is the world he
wanted us to have. *I want to come in your mouth.*
It was uncertain just whom he addressed.

There are things one would rather not know.
I had intended for this recollection to be modest—
but it would not be right to not tell you how
when we were together once, he told me,
very clearly, that my technique would not do.
This is not the worst thing I could tell you.

All My Wives

When I say my wives are cages, I don't mean I'm a bird.
Collapsible shelves, they hide their usefulness when not
in use. All my wives contain terrariums: terrible and fetid
atmospheres in which their salamander selves linger atop
damp rocks. Their hands are damp as the tissues they ball
in their hands, though none of my wives could make a fist,
not even if I asked, no, not even if I commanded them to,

an amusing idea I must someday revisit. My wives are like
the Small Mammal House at the zoo, their rooms kept dark
so visitors may view their nocturnal truths, that anonymous
wakefulness we sleepers do not care to know. None of my
wives are like lanterns, nor do their ribs sing with canaries.
It does my wives good to run my errands, for it keeps them
purposeful. I do not allow pockets on their shirts or skirts.

Theirs are unforgiving interiors. A woman's hands should
always be in plain sight, preferably chafed from dishwater
and cold. A woman's hands should be kept raw from wind
and sewing. When I want my wives to come out, I turn off
the lights and crouch to listen as they compare me: *Who do
I smack more often? Whom shall I take for my queen?* They think
I take pleasure in belaboring this decision, yet to think of it

is to imagine I might some day purchase a book I've never
desired to read. When I snap the lights on, they scatter like
roaches. Why read when there are so many worried brows

upon which to set the delicate glass of my gaze down? One
of my wives petitioned, once. One of them dared to cry.
They've tried to make me sad with their eyes. Let them try.
I would rather buy a hat, a walking stick, move alone within

my chamber, pose before my mirror. I do not need a queen,
I do not like tantrums. At times, I shudder, alone in my bed,
when I consider how their desires must churn like the onset
of inclement weather. They could be one, she could be one-
hundred. I just saw her shadow skulking down the walk. She's
drunk, as usual. Her shakes, her heart-murmurs, her general
unease. Pity the creature. She has a disease. If it gets worse,

I'll be forced to consider treatment. All my wives have four
legs each. What we call arms may as well be legs, so it seems
to me as I kneel behind each, not knowing one from the other,
only their asses' moon-curves aglow in lamplight. With such
anonymity, we are pleasured. It would not do for them to undo
the tiny latches, the wire doors to their cages. It would not do
to lift the lids of their terrariums. Something untoward might

escape, roam the grounds. For then I should be afraid to walk
alone at night, my new hat atop my clean head, walking stick
in hand, as I move onward, staking out crevices, damp places
that lock my eyes: the fragrant earth I move atop my inheritance,
the herd of them breathing behind me in the dark. At the thrill
of their whispers, I stick my stick into the ground, turn on my
boot's heel. My wife, on her four legs, waits quietly in the hay.

Your Call Is Very Important to Us

Which is why when we call you we keen,
so you may shake harder in your waiting,
and should you question whether it is true,
you'll learn from your longing how very

important we find you. So when our morning
drops blue upon your head, then swings itself
against your eyes like a lead pipe, then presses
your worried brow with soothing, cottony

clouds of light, you'll wake at last from
your fever, your fright, and know you knew
we'd call, that you've been waiting for us
all along. Then we'll call back, shriller still,

for what is an audience that does not cry back?
Whose lover dares to hold back?
Who loves and will not answer the phone?
So when we drop night's block on your head

as a door loves to slam a hand in its jamb,
when we land beneath your heel, our stars
shards of glass left unswept on a floor,
you are only waiting for our call.

You knew it had to be us all along. We love
your alertness to the sky, your painful *Why?*

Your somber way of walking yourself home
alone. If not for our siren cry, what would

you do? How else could you believe anyone,
anyone at all, cares about you? Here, have
a drink on us; we'll have a drink on you.
Your taxi has left. Your home is ransacked.

We would ask that you not cry out. We would
ask you not to speak, although we speak to you.
You will consider the back door a distant country.
Know we can reach *at least* that far to find you.

Muckraker

As one in dowte, thys ys my ssayyng:
Have I dysplesed yow in any thyng?
—Thomas Wyatt

That greasy letter into which my legs entered,
its tone conspiratorial as his wink, a linguistic
wriggling of the eyebrows, a *heh-heh*—it may
as well have appeared before my door chafing
the air with the stiff noise of its cheap leather
jacket. Am I not chagrined by his proposition
to put it all behind us and begin again as friends?
How do I reply? And how shall I contend with
the fact, Reader, that this matter cannot mean
much to you, and that I, as author, am required

to consider how to tell this tale in a manner that
will entertain you, despite having never met you
and having no way of knowing how to affect you,
get you to let me touch you all over, kiss your lips
then tongue your mouth open, move my mouth
down your neck to the valley of your chest, pluck
buttons off you with my teeth. I have thought of
this for a great, long time. I have sat here hunched,
feeling sick; I have paced rugs bare. Why should
you care? His door opened, selves spilled out my

heart's bucket, flopped their silvers across a floor.
He was too poor to enter a store, too poor to pay
postage for a letter, so poor he'd have stolen crumbs

from a mouse, so poor he'd have sold his cadaver
if he could. Yet, consider the man: his deep voice
began to work away at my inhibitions like sandpaper.
Before I knew it, I'd moved right into him, wiped
the eyes of windows clear, mended the tears in his
screens, made our bed with sheets so icy clean—
but you do not want me to give too much away.

What fun would that be? Here, as with any tale,
the moral's like a molar, set far back in the mouth
of the story. Open wider, let me stick my pliers in,
wrench it out. Left unattended, anything's prone
to spoil, go bad, turn rotten, sink into itself, stink
up the whole house. And how shall I begin to make
my account? Dig through the junk heap. Start small.
He grew over me calmly as a vine climbs a trellis.
Your nightgown is unbecoming. A few small terrorisms.
Eyes wide at my wince, incredulous. *You thought I'd*

hit you? Loom large. His question was rhetorical.
You have a disease. Or aim dead center and toss my
dart. Tell it plain, an expensive watch, rent checks,
designer sunglasses, a ring, a student named Nadine,
Prozac, Visa, Harold Bloom, Jim Beam. But this is not
the stuff of poesy, is it? Shall I shut up and return to
my book? Details! Only details can raise this story's
sail. Money's one thing, but this is another poverty
altogether. We had an agreement, pills plucked daily
from a dial. Lawns in August, plot after plot of green,

the warm hiss of sprinklers arcing rainbows, children's
delighted screams. It was a fault to desire these things.
Junk heap! Wrench the cumbersome thing out, heavy
and foul as a discarded couch, his omission. Hadn't
I known his books were his children? Adding up all
the hours I'd breathed beside him, years handed over
as if on a platter, it is simply too much, all that while,
how each night he partook of his clean, black sleep—
Reader, do I border on the obscene? Have I forced
you to give up your sympathies in exchange for more

lurid curiosities? I am reminded of a trip I took long
ago to a small city in Mexico. How carefully I listened
to a man tell us the only means by which to recognize
real silver was from a number stamped on the jewelry's
side. Only later, arriving home, would I realize that
lowly guide contrived to have the van arrive at stores
run by his friends, bracelets and rings sweating off
their dull green circlets onto my wrists, my fingers.
Counterfeit! This is war, this is two spiders a child's
dropped into a jar, scrabbling at the glass and flinging

their webs, each so intent on killing the other, the fact
they are both trapped has ceased to matter. *O, blood,
blood, blood!* Shall I, Reader, be a tad more explicit?
Here's my problem: I must be very, very careful with
what I say. He always complained that I caused a *scene*—
even at the courthouse, after I'd paid the processing
fee, when asked whether he could spare some change

35

to pay the parking attendant, he growled *Keep your voice down* as if it had jumped on his legs. To speak of money in public is impolite, or so his mother had taught him.

His wisdom tooth was rotting, the infection was liable to spread to his brain, and he was too poor to have it extracted. He stated this over and over, slowly, as if he believed I was having trouble understanding English or had suddenly turned mentally deficient. A problem: If you can't trust people, you can't trust books, since books are people and people are books. Shall I ask him to sign it? *Beautiful dreamer, may all your beginnings be true beginnings.* You think this unseemly for me to confide? Reader, don't mistake me for someone who gives a shit, or your bride. I have no loyalty and I have no pride.

Your Childhood

I.

Years later, frozen at a curb, atilt before the traffic's
loud blur, preparing to launch into the street deep
with technicolor chromes and lose myself to the legs
tangling forth, even now, I can spy it limping across
the horizon's tired red that rests its lip just beyond
the farthest line of my vision, can see it scuttle off
into the safety of the softly shadowed mouth of an
alleyway. What's next? Yesterday, the sign it lugged
begged for bus fare. Today, it wears a cast fashioned
from newspaper. Tomorrow, it'll ask if I have change
for a nickel. And tonight, somewhere beneath a soiled
rumple of cardboard spongy with rainwater, lies your
scheming childhood, hatching up more pitiful plans.

II.

Your childhood and I go way back. Remember when
it put its finger down my throat when I got too drunk
to walk? We slipped those tubes of pink lipstick up our
sleeves at the shopping mall, we chewed nicorette while
smoking. I picked it up hitchhiking: its mouth tugged on
a joint as it bragged that it wanted you dead. It got off
wherever I planned to head, said anywhere was where
it planned to end up. Though it never paid for gas, it

knew a trick or two, thought I wasn't looking as it picked
through my purse, and later fingered lovingly my driver's
license. Your childhood wants my childhood, makes out
with my yearbook photo, jacks off to my high school
journal; it comes to love my parents more than I do.

III.

Your childhood turns up viscous in my soup, floats
its pale residue of congealed bacon fat, seals every
meal's surface. Saying *I'm not hungry* translates into
you don't know what it means to go hungry. Standing
in the grocery store's checkout line, it's aghast I'm
buying boneless chicken breasts. It would have me
strip down, flinch beneath the fluorescence, offer up
every last inch of my clothing. Marching up to gather
my garments into its arms, it announces that I'll find
them at the Salvation Army, then strides out between
the electric doors muttering that *Some people don't
know how good they have it*. Even when forced to eat
dog food, your childhood was never so ungrateful.

IV.

Your childhood prying open a can, your childhood
waking you because it's afraid of the dark. For years.
Of the yellowing polar bear at that dank zoo that will
not stop banging its head against the concrete floe of

its habitat, you alone know the briny depths of its woe. Once, your school sent a letter home stating it'd found you *gifted*. Your mother crumpled it up. The ranging plains, the dust-strewn land on which you grew. How could anyone know what it was to grow up as you? If it had its way, your childhood would smother her, heft her to a rank ravine's devouring grasses. Hate's her opium. You don't mind when your voice makes a face flinch. Maybe you like it. Your childhood's seen to that.

Alibi Poem

The alibi checks out:
From the hotel room.
Ladies in short skirts
in the hotel's lobby.
Tells us where it was,
just what exactly it
was doing when the
unspeakable began:

Slowing down an avalanche, fast-forwarding a glacier, conducting bathroom
surgery on its finger, plucking someone's lights out, stun-gunning a crowd
of pedestrians, mesmerizing the eye of a barroom brawl, collecting various
replicas of its father, defrosting an icebox, acquiring yet another venereal
disease, balancing its checkbook, inflating its grades, seducing its students,
stalking its stalker, scraping dog shit off the sole of its shoe, assuming a fetal
position, acquiring an assassin, going undercover, drinking alone, organizing
cutlery, selling its prized stamp collection, opening its eyes inside its waters.

Burning its furniture, memorizing lighthouses, applauding the riots, looting
storefronts, reversing its baptism, losing its grammar, adoring its cell phone,
entering its gates of heaven, taste-testing toothpaste, flirting with its cavities,
taking a lungful, divining its weather, recalling its vote, shopping for oranges,
singing off-key, polishing its karma, dealing its cards, leaving the casino after
dawn, gargling Lysol, reading the Classics, changing a light bulb, eschewing
materialism, arresting its fellow citizens, avoiding the newspaper, creating its
binary, joining the opposition and—when it had a spare moment—weeping.

Painting its nails gold, being put under, considering liposuction, sleeping on the ferry, rolling its own cigarettes, reviling its childhood, then verbalizing its prejudices, falling down on dance floors, knocking up its knees, threatening a mountain range, attempting boredom, imploding with evidence, weathering your merry-go-round, seducing the turnpike, courting a satellite, courting its dog walker, seducing a court room, sucking off the court transcriber, serving as its own lawyer, giving birth to its own litter, calling a certain park bench *Son,* waking up next to its version of Hemingway, wishing itself stillborn.

Little Poem That Tries

Little Poem That Tries likes to make pretend it is a land
where dislikes inform its borders, tells its knees to leave
if they won't stop kneeling, then announces it's time to

my Kentucky courthouse heart my credit counseling heart

clean house. Its orders come from the top, shudder their
way down, striking fear into the bowels of the lowliest
custodial workers. Appoints serial killers for its customs

my file for bankruptcy heart my long distance phone call

officials. Destroys its orange groves with a single dream.
Reenters the house, limping. Acquires an endless supply
of Xanax, believes it possible it is living inside a movie

heart my courtesy call heart my manual dial my I am dying

and when the sun calms down—if the fervent sun ever
calms itself down—it'll pat itself on the back, think how
much prettier the days are with the companion of a sun

heart my note in my throat tries and dies heart my Jersey

that kills: how in drought graves split open, cannot keep
their bones down. The land's heated disarray underneath
such violet skies; does it not remind one of a tangled sheet,

Turnpike heart my Divorce Court heart my small claims

how the pill of the past is easy enough to swallow once
it's crushed up, spoon-fed with such amorous light?
To gaze all day as the sun plays along a riot of graves . . .

heart my service window heart my claimant heart my

rather a peaceful pastime, as if what's been said is truly
done. Though it never intended to undertake a coup, one
might conclude from the teary countenances of officials

hit my car heart my notarized heart my foreclosed heart

round the conference table that the Little Poem That Tries
was never right for this job in the first place. After it pats
its reader down, it slips into a hired car, makes itself *far*,

my unsubsidized loan heart my on loan and lonely heart

makes itself *away*. Now, the hot, purpling sky turns to fog.
All the scorched fields shrink below. The still stars above.
And Little Poem That Tries snows and snows and snows.

my how could you have hit the one nice thing I owned heart

Postscript

We sure are tired, so long's the longing
we undertook. It would put you to sleep
to read the book of examinations, trials,
and speculations. Even the cattle minded
the haul we had in mind for them, lugging
the same records across and back the same
lands, as if we were lost in the ocean.
The cry-me scarves were sold on the way,
blue silk soaked with tear-salt; the fire
ants we played with for pain, arguing
whose hands had become the numbest, lost.
It is sorry, then, the haul come to nothing
in the net, only more weight of pages
and pages to trod with upon our backs.
Though the goal was not known, we knew
it would be discovered, would bloom out
like hills of poppies, crossing our eyes
with their red scent—though the idea, if not
the goal, was always in plain-eyed view.
To turn the ear like a weather antenna,
risk the tamper of satellite communications,
to yelp like puppies in an abandoned basket,
to scream like dirt to an eye that endeavors
to clean. If someday you should have the sense
to find us, camped still at the place we stopped
to rest, where resting took longer than any
of us could expect, do not be drawn

by our gypsy calls, our lonely tweaking
at guitar strings, do not pause for a listen:
we have nothing more to sing of you.

Lying My Head Off

Here's my head, in a dank corner of the yard.
I lied it off and so off it rolled.
It wasn't unbelieving that caused it
to drop off my neck and loll down a slope.
Perhaps it had a mind of its own, wanted
to leave me for a little while.

Or it was scared and detached itself
from the stalk of my neck as a lizard's tail
will desert its body in fright of being caught.
The fact is, I never lied. The fact is,
I always lied. Before us, we have two mirrors.
At times, they say, one must lie in order

to survive. I drove by the house, passed
it several times, pretending it was not
my own. Its windows were red with curtains
and the honeyed light cast on the porch
did not succeed in luring me back inside.
I never lied. I drove by the house,

suckling the thought of other lovers
like a lozenge. I was pale as a papery birch.
I was pure as a brand new pair of underwear.
It will be a long while before I touch another.
Yet, I always lied, an oil slick on my tongue.
I used to think that I was wrong, could

not tell the truth for what it was. Yet, one
cannot take a lawsuit out on oneself.
I would have sworn in court that I believed
myself and then felt guilty a long time after.
I hated the house and I hated myself.
The house fattened with books, made me

grow to hate books, when all the while
it was only books that never claimed
to tell the truth. I hated him and I hated
his room, within which his cloud of smoke
heaved. I disappeared up narrow stairs,
slipped quick beneath the covers.

My stomach hurts, I told him, I was tired.
I grew my dreams thick through hot nights:
dear, flickering flowers. They had eyes
which stared, and I found I could not afford
their nurture, could not return their stare.
Meanwhile, liars began their parade

without my asking, strode sidewalks inches
before my doorstep. I watched their hulking
and strange beauty, their songs pregnant
with freedom, and became an other self.
I taught children how to curse.
I bought children gold pints of liquor.

I sold my mind on the street.
I learned another language. It translates easily.

Here's how: *What I say is not what I mean,*
nor is it ever what I meant to say.
You must not believe me when I say
there's nothing left to love in this world.

Part II

Fragment of the Head of a Queen

I.

Gesture

Have you known the roar of an estranging city,
freeways braided round the head's dome, traffic
a throbbing wound to the ear, you have seen
genderless ancients wade through mild rivulets
of shadow that pass beneath overpasses, pick
through peelings of houses, finding gold only
in the yellowed rinds shucked from oranges.
As they sift for treasure shed from our rooms,
I fall to love a thought: my ghastly head raised.
But this species of story makes of one a servant.
Have you known the roar of an estranging city,
is only another way of saying, *I was defeated.*

II.

Translation

Behold your head, a hive the bear's pawed down
from its bough, smashed to ground for sweetness,
honey leaking a yellow jasper. Its furious center
dispelled, now all of you is leaving. This is how
the self turns on self, goes vagabond, this is how

you are repaid for your industry. Their domicile
dismantled, thoughts now roam the air like aimless
troops, seeking recompense in the sticky jewels
of an empty soda can, crawl into its lip's sweet
keyhole, cannot make their way back out the dark.
I would have made for them a freedom song, if
the teller of this story had only a slave's loyalty.

III.

Rupture

Once, to gaze was to taste an eye's persimmon,
a true fruit shucked from its skin with a glance.
The very manner her mouth gave way to display
the white seeds of teeth *was* flesh, too permissive.
A thumb pressed hard to her cheek left its petal.
Irises, twin grapes, too ripe with light, raptured
to be plucked, stomped, bottled. Had we left her
to froth and ferment, she might have drank herself.
Or is it merely that beauty reciprocates violence.
One becomes indentured to a story's riddle.
Loved overmuch, she preferred to be loathed.
It comforts us to believe this is what she chose.

Mug Shot

Face a distortion. Expression falling back into distance,
as a crowd recedes behind a fleeing man. Iris's brown
black back at the flash, and a hoard of curses perched
on the brink of lip. The mouth cruelly fixed and stained
with an outline of dark lipstick, and in her eyes a light
stirred with the throb of siren's pulse, its mix of glee
and negligence an affront to any decent citizen. A face
crumbling like an old shed begging to be knocked down

with a single kick. Eyes roaming the room as one surveys
land standing neck-deep in a pit, whisky-pitched, ether-lit.
This, as a whole, pulled into the second's suck of lens:
while mirth crawled the halls of countenance, sorrows
flowered behind the brow, and a deadly apathy took up
residence, a serious and true crime was being planned.

A Brief Attachment

I regard your affections, find your teeth have
left me a bruise necklace. Those lipstick
    marks leech a trail, ear to ear, facsimile your
smile. Your 40 ounces of malt liquor, your
shrink hate, your eyes dialing 911. The hearts
you draw with ballpoint on my cigarette packs
    when I've left the room, penned in your girl's

cursive, look demented, misshapen approximations
of what I refuse to hand over. It's a nice touch,
    though: a little love to accompany the cancer.
    My thought follows you to where you spend
your days lying in bed, smoking and reading
the Beats. The accumulation of clothes and ashes
    circles you, rising like a moat after rainfall.

Often you are a study in detachment—the trigger
eye is your eye, still as a finger poised to press
    should one refuse to cooperate, and I wonder
    how you can hate men so much when you think
like one. Think of what I could be doing outside
if I could unlock the door of myself: think bikini,
    think soda fountain, think tradition, a day lacking

entirely your brand of ambivalence. If you were
a number, I'd subtract you; if you were a sentence,
    I'd rewrite you. Are you the one who left these

wilted flowers, are you the one whose PIN spells
out H-O-L-E? Why are you wearing my clothes?
If you are weather, then I'm a town, closing down
    at word of your coming: you're a glacier on fast

forward, you're direct as a detour, when I say
good-bye you move in next door. You say you
    want to have my baby, you want to buy me a car,
    and you're too young to enter a bar. I should tether
you to a tree in the dark park, allow the moon to stroke
your white neck. I should give you a diamond collar,
    walk you around the block and show you off.

"Practically an Orphan"

This is not about them, but what happens to them.
Pick a brick, a plastic bag, a gun, or any instrument
heavy with intent, since you are heavy in intent on
forgetting them. This is not about their good faces,
or about how it will happen while they sleep. Not
about their knickknacks, the flowers cut fresh from
their garden to stand tall in a vase, nor the metallic
sheen of a scrubbed basin that is their kitchen sink.

Gravity kills, not us. How else can a hammer fall?
There's more than one way to cut a person off mid
speech. Open the refrigerator of the heart and sniff—
something's gone bad in the blood. Not about what
they are, were, will not be again. Streets, remember?
Paved for you to choose a wrong, a right. Preferably
smothered, putting goose-down to good use. Gravity
helps hands fall, pulls them down to press. *Regret?*

The axe fell to their faces as a magnet pulls at magnet.
The pillow lay like lead atop their heads, its feathers
rustling with excitement. The gun's nose butted my
hand like a friendly dog. But my most beautiful day
was the first I had alone. The metal case swung from
my hand, as I walked beneath the kindest light I've
known; it said: *the future*. Why should you look so
sad all of a sudden? We'll laugh all night, we'll wash

our knives at a river's edge. When once lonely, only children, we wandered the estates of our minds; how badly we wished to set those coarse grasses on fire, only to find our matches too damp to strike. Unfold yourself beneath this willow, screw your arms out their sockets, take down the tent of yourself. We're done with this childhood. We'll lie limp forever and ever, forgive ourselves every wrong thing we've done.

Coup de Soleil

I.

He hands down the sun. He picks our planet's lock.
The stars perch on his outstretched arm, sides sharp
as beaks. Swung out into flight, they carry his word's
weight. They return, claws clutching the stricken
rabbit's carcass. He skins it with a glance, roasts
it over a pyre. He skins us of our clothes and we
lie across the plate of his bed's porcelain spread.
He makes of us a meal, he picks our bones clean.

Up and down and all over the hills we run our hands,
and the sun comes down so hard that looking at him
is drinking fire from the cups of eyes. We once knew
him wheat, a gold square of pasture eyed from miles
above. Gold: we loved to look down, sink to linger.
Sun-struck, sunstroke, our long illness now begins.
How fever writhes the thatched roof of this house.
How by the end he hasn't untouched one bit of us.

II.

Three blood drops on the snow, ink stains welled up
on a handkerchief. A falcon wounds a wild goose, so
three drops of blood fall on the snow. Frozen in his
saddle, spear held erect, his posture expressed hostile

challenge. It's said by memory's complexion he was
transfixed: lip's rose embroidering body's white sheet.
They broke his trance by draping a yellow scarf over
the drops. They gave him back to war and reason.

And the sun comes down so hard when looking at him—
as an image is struck onto the face of a coin, the eye
sends its beam into the beholder's eye, striking the face
into dismay, knocking out whole hunks of wall till all
that's left is rubble and dust. Wooly clouds of smoke
pile up in the sky. Troops menace a horizon.
Three gold hairs caught by the teeth of his comb.
I would not exchange them for the Empire of Rome.

III.

A historic hotel is the setting for the hysteria that ensues
once those yellow notes are plucked from his throat.
A falcon wounds a wild goose, three drops of blood fall
on the snow. We lay our cards out on clean sheets, sip
gin and play rummy. I don't know how to play, so how
can I win? Whose bluff is whose. Ours is a classic drama,
tears pulled like strings from the eyes. I'd never slept
in a room so fine, on such a bed, so soft and high, never

began to think I'd lose my mind over a good-bye, O,
the many tears plopping into a chalice. He picked the stars
up and screwed their bulbs back into the sky! I've locked
myself inside the bathroom, drunk chilled vodka straight

from the bottle. He's at the door, knocking gold flakes
off his knuckles. Three gold hairs, the teeth of his comb.
I would not exchange them for a cartload of emeralds
or carbuncles. The floor's cool tiles. My fever's begun.

The Unfortunates

occupy the corners where cars spill off
highways, work the vehicles halted before
traffic lights, heft limbs that look screwed
on wrong, hang juice cartons fashioned into
receptacles for change from their necks with
shoestrings, peer into windows to find our
eyes with looks like keys trying out locks
for the right fit. Stopped, one eye restless
on the light's red, the other transfixed by
a leg grown so wrong we twist inwardly at
the approach of it, we wary of their intent
to snatch our pity like a purse. When they
bend to the glass, we clutch our sympathies,
close the face like a door. But they are not
thieves, they work for this: it is their job to
stagger around on sticks. Trading on woeful
expression, exchanging pities for pennies,
shaming us with their disfigurements: I will
not give them a cent.
    Nights I hand myself
over to the dull roar of the city's motor, lie
like an amputee and count my ghost limbs,
eyelids clamped tight against a streetlight's
dampening flicker. The floorboards vibrate
with a neighbor's obscenities, malice moves
like mice in the walls, and to sleep is to live
inside an hour with jeweled beasts, the heart

thinking itself some priceless rock briefly
released from the dark safety of its locked
cabinet. But in sleep nothing is noble, our
streets of mind crowded with vendors whose
stalls are stacked with misfortunes arranged
neatly as produce. Those hours we haggle,
wondering when the sincerity of sky's blue
will arrive, how come nobody's bothered to
repair the loose latch on the front gate, and
what kinds of eyes melancholy lovers have.

Stone Fruit

A train ran   along the track   its pale embankment
by a building with a hundred   balconies as blue as false
blue eyes are   That was the year I   Probably still drunk
the noon after   face a fingerprint pressed   oily surface
I expected great things   You could read all about them
My tongue delivered   a newspaper   onto the grassy slick
of your front lawn   I took out a savings account   I made no friends

I sat in a cafeteria   worrying my face   might lurch
every breath   clinking into a piggy bank   An important man's
hand   furtive   scurried down my spine while   his secretary
looked away   He cured cancer   I typed it   from dictation
I thought I was   You could read all about it   important
What a long   ago   left my expression scratched on
plexiglass   Slipped a tiny tape into the machine's slot   pressed

a pedal   his voice oozed a letter   I wanted you   a pit to peach
beneath my sheets   to eat   away at the bedding   get to you
at its center   You could read all about it   Like a rodent
rummaging   through the liquor cabinet   Hurt my hands
letter after letter   his voice a snail   emerging from its shell
I wanted you   you know   enough already   Hands on weekends
extended to perform a jitter on the train   at behest of their delicate

hangover   A hand left   on the train's seat   misplaced
like a mitten   An important man's hand   foraged my neckline
His voice's slug slugging its passage along   my ear's canal

63

I counted my plots before   they hatched I put all my bombs
in one briefcase   As missions go it   was poorly executed
As far as making   no friends   opening a savings account
I expected great things   That worthless long ago   read all about it

How a lake appeared   its shine a lemon at dusk   a scented coin
passed beneath   the bank teller's   scratched plexiglass   partition
A girl dredged   at its edge   I wanted you like the moon never
wanted to come   in the first place   Had better things to do
would rather   read the paper than peer   before us with its
pocked face   Hands touch   as if just hatched and   stumbling
new into this world   my face in a cafeteria   worrying its features

tending to tics as if   they might be triggered   Blue balconies
empty but for sun-chairs   no body standing   before wintry sun
You will or won't   read about it at all   the train lurching into
the station   where people get off   Saving my account
with words   encoding it as one embroidered   this discreet rose
onto this velvet pillowcase   To lean against   to unfold unto
to be important   to be the girl at the lake   make your   nice home

nice   to kiss the important doctor   once he agrees to   cure me
of this   Then to forgo   the moon's dismal features   slap my
body down on your lawn   its entry entire   entreaty   Good-bye
a stick of dynamite tied to its tail   Now omit the girl entry   lake
entry   replace them so   you may view my hands   in our museum
in their new glass case   Nothing is news or new   I wanted to
take the train to you   detonate my face   be your obituary.

Orange Drink Man

See me stand inside my bedroom's lantern,
climb your eyes three stories high, to where
there's just air and a thin screen between us.
See me watch from inside my window's lit
eye: you lurching across the Quik-Trip lot,
the pedestrians moving around your howl,
mouth opening its purse full of dingy coins,
hair a sooty brush rising wild on your head,
a liter of plastic sun clutched in your hands.

Your wrist leaves its cuff of tattered flannel
to raise the plastic jug, your lips pulling at
the dying fizz, you oblivious to our minutes
together, just mesh and a mile of air between
us. An empty space is your friend: you pat it
on the back. You pat it again and laugh, walk
toward the park too dark with trees for me,
where you live like a jungle cat in the wood's
safe clasp with your neighbor, Bicycle Man.

When the town lays the last of its dark down,
and light seeps deep into the cracks of edifice,
disappearing like evidence, you leak back out
into the streets. See me lit from behind, stand
before the window in my kitchen: I have made
you my business, registered your movements
within walls so thin the neighbors can hear me

blink as I conduct upon your drama my sad
arithmetic, trying to make you make sense.

Though no one's ever seen you eat, I know
your ribs don't show, since I saw you raise
your shirt in the lot's tarry heat to fan your
thick torso, its male line of hair, for a moment,
exposed. You did not see me. I looked away.
See me stand in this room's incandescence,
trammeling your streets with my stare. Set
me by your sun, let your sun set me, let me
walk up into your eye, carrying my suitcase.

Flowers, Always

Inexplicable, the sign outside a deli scrawled
with FLOWERS
                and below that: ALWAYS.
But there were no flowers. And I have never
seen an Always. I would like to,
                and I have looked.
I have kept my eye keen
                for Always, have liked
its idea like an expensive purse, coveting it as
it appears,
            riding the arms of rich ladies who are
so very lady.   I've rolled on velvet
        cushions where I heard Always slept,
and I once tried to kiss Always,
           but I don't think it was the Always
I was looking for.
I like your Always, it looks
such a demanding pet. It looks like it kisses
nice and soft.
              It looks like the bruise I found
flowering on my knee.
               I fell down at your voice.
Not to worry, I got right back up, walked ten
more blocks
           and by then I was halfway home.
I knock my knees blue
             and scabbed crawling

toward you, wanting flowers,

       and always, always, always
to slide against the cold vinyl of a car's seat,
your pale hands

       on the bare backs of my legs,
that's one Always I want, and whoever knew
there were so many species

       of Always? Your bare hands
on the pale backs

       of my thighs, printing bruise,
and if you said *Flowers*, said *Always* and we
could erect a forever

       of something like sheets
       and breakfast and an ordinary
day, my eyes would

       always slide across the table toward
you,

    to warm their twin marbles in your palm,
my face would flower

       for you daily, so that when we
die, roses might petal

       themselves out our throats.

Landscape with Hungry Girls

There's blood here. The skyline teethes the clouds
raw and rain's course streams a million umbilical
cords down windows and walls. Everything gnaws,
and the pink polish on their girl-nails chips, flakes
off as they continue to dig through towering heaps
of refuse. It's a story, as usual. As usual, a phone
and dead silence. Or the phone: a lobster to the ear.
Girls resigned to being girls. The softer faces they
find in the mirrors. The limp shake, a hand placed,
a flower wilting moist on the man's palm. Or hard
handshakes deemed "aggressive": snakes. O, girls.
All of them carefully watching carefully the faces
of their sleeping men, even when their own faces are
more beautiful in their watching, and if only they'd
watch their own faces beneath the revolving lights
sliding between the blinds: they are blinded from
watching their men sleep so dumbly. The headaches,
the insistent grip of a gnawing stomach, eating itself.
Thinking hunger is strength, how hurt they are, girls
picking at food on their plates. *I like a girl who eats.*
Careful, what you say you want. The moon is distant,
yet cousin to her face: our genders worse than alien.
Bleeding is something everyone does. You don't call.
Girls snack on skyscrapers, girls gut their teddy bears,
and girls saw their own faces off. What is it to lack
compassion? When you walk through a zoo do you
not think the animals it houses could have been you?

69

Who would you be, how hungry, if you were a girl
feeding only on the meek sleep of male countenance?
Would you stand vigil, would you starve as they do?

Pretty Speech (The Occasion of Your Death)

When you died, phones clattered off ears to tiled floors
as phones in movies do. Everyone gasped, no one could
breathe. There was a scream. I grew ugly from a distance
at the clabber of your boots scuffing rock wall. You always
knew how to cause a scene. A scream. Forgive me, your
error was obscene. You, unlatched over air eight-hundred
feet deep. Even my parents paused their DVD. Descent
swift, lousy Icarus. Forgive me for being mean. You know
how it is. When that old Arctic feeling comes over me, it's
extreme. Keeping up appearances makes me pathological.
Your death, I've been reading about it. The accounts are
practically mythological. I'm more likely to marry a stranger
than believe that your cousin, who was on the scene, found,
as he claims, your necklace snagged on gray granite and will
always wonder if some greater force led him to it. I mean,
please. Dead? You're lucky you missed the memorial service.
The spiritual director directed us to wave our arms in unison
above our heads to guide you toward the heavens, in case
you got lost, I guess. I'll admit, I was a little pissed. I asked
to read a poem. Pastor Mary Cornfed took the folded page
from my hands, unfolded it, glanced, and then deemed it
inappropriate, as it was *awfully intimate*. (See pages 58–60.)
The faith-healing cunt. I've been in a bad mood ever since.

Catatonia

Knock down the tree your head is in. The ball of it
kicked too high, it rattles precarious, looks lodged
deep in its crook of a bough, dull among the glittering
things tangled in the hair of leaves and twigs. On each
green finger, soda can rings. Tree, rain down your
metal petals, release the broken basket where

I last kept my face. Tonight, the moon looked over,
a rose swimming astride the clouds steaming above
the skyline. It'd been so long since I noticed the sky,
since I used my eyes, I startled as when seeing an old
friend on the street. Yet while my vision could smell
the familiar, it found the face turning back at my

my yell a stranger's. His face blurred as a moon, his
hands rattling deep in the pods of his pockets. And
was it not him? From behind, from aside, from across
the traffic, from my window above: surely I did not
mistake his movement for another's? Turning sharp
corners in that way I know, as a blade skins an apple.

When I step out from the house, my neighbors' eyes
skin me with malice. The magnolia's cloaked the walk
with its petals, made a fragrant path of bruise. It hurts
to walk over beauty. Indulge me the excuse of a solitary
childhood, a temperament that was at once discerned
temperamental, my neck's stalk weak with the weight

of my head's dolorous flower, heavy through summer.
If I see him again, how shall I know him? Mouth first
a jewel, then a jeweled scabbard, his knife then running
smooth against my throat. Spray of wisteria, spray of
the slashed jugular petaling out its roses along the walk.
I held still, tasted metal. Vacuous and taut with its airy

thoughts, it rose quickly, lifted itself up into the air as
if with invisible arms. Shall I replace it with the head
of a horse, make myself a centaur in reverse? Shall I call
the fire department, ask them to ladder it down? Must
I watch the twigs combing my black hair until the stars
are thumbed shut by dawn and my startled eyes close?

NyQuil

What a mother of a cloud the sky
      has dumped on us tonight: a pig fat
with fleece, adrowse in its dankness,
      suspended above us like a Zeppelin
fattening on the verge—I lie wet

as stripped flesh, open to the fog
      that drapes my window with gauze,
begging for a sleep thick as syrup.
      A clock types, a typewriter winds
backward through old scrolls, humming

its melancholy distraction. Green bottle
      languishing in the cabinet, you want
my veins pulled though with wire
      of bluish fire: *Dreams of parrots*
await you, a slumber to outnumber

all waking days awaits you. The day,
      all its doings and dids, unravels its
ill-fitting sweater, as the sweetness
      burns through the tongue, sinks past
heart to ignite a tiny fire in the belly's

cave. It makes a bright hollow. It shuts
      the latch of throat, smoothes breath out
so it may pass lips without catching

on gasp. I thrash up from bed, cough
until out my mouth bursts green feathers,

and I cough all the parrots out. I cough
        up childhood, its roller skates, its curled
grubs tucked wet in matted leaves. Now,
        another slipper, a finger, a nip, again
a sip of that platonic kiss. Dousing all

my coughs out. Cool sheets cusp my
        neck: mother's hand. I am forgetting him
and I am forgetting them. Wait a long
        while before you find my face, wait before
you slap me awake with patient sunlight.

Mushrooms

Pale caps erect as chiseled stone make the mind
a sculpture garden. Staking their luminous flags
on the damp nap of lawn, they blazon a ghostly
vulnerability, are obvious as the pointed question
the face cannot master, its flush climbing the neck
and cloaking cheeks with admission. Nocturnal
and explicit as greed, their presence suggestive
as a door left ajar, their appearance is so sudden
my mouth makes an O. What moon tugs these
clean sheets straight up from soil? Their skin
bare there as skin is bare everywhere after clocks
hand us down hallways, and our mouths lock.

Monsterful

We meet day-plain and inches away, faces
facing off in a garden,

                  kissing closed kisses,
solemn, bone-dry, and exquisite as the leaves
of our sweating faces

                  glisten, sheens giving
back each tree's green. *My greenery grows
untoward,*

                  *branches burst windows, menace
doors, what sky is wide enough to house me?*
                  Breath labored, we meet
between noon and never,
in heat dense and coupled with rose scent.

                  Koi rise mouth-first
in a fountain's deep basin, bodies bone-white
and rust-flecked,

                  worn as worn dress gloves,
whiskered gapes funneling the water's glossy
surface. You water

                  my eyes with your eyes
and the plant of my gaze   climbs toward
your sky, wanting your mouth

                  to hatch into mine,
as a cloud contracts inside this evening's sky.
                  Nights have me now think of how
we first met, not pressed

                  inside dream's tent,

but day-bright,   mouths soft as opiates.
In a gold pool poured

                   out your lit window,
chained to this lingering,
I stand so still my skin feels each spore settle.
To slip like a vapor

           beneath your door, appear
in the cloud your breath presses to a mirror,

           to read an evening paper
in your heart's anteroom. Necking in a cloud
bank,

      milking an hour's dew, hands roving
their devouring herd,

      you tongued my every sharp blade
soft, and I knew   the terrible suspense
of a hand's white claw push open

       the heavy lid of my chest,
emerge a night terror: I have conceived
an impossible child,

      now catalogue your words' hues
by density of violet, become altogether new
    and newly violent.

A Fainting Couch

I could have slept years on it, my cracked book
resting its small ship of words atop my breasts,
lulled near to sleep by my sea-breath, lowering
and rising with the heave of my chest: narrative
leaking its indiscretions in between those folds
where my blouse buttoned, characters lowering
themselves, rung by rung, to fall at the bottom
of that dim chamber where love was once said
to happen, a cave lit low by the faint gaslight
cast from their lanterns. Towering down from
its roof, the stalagmites, sentiment wax-crafted,
must have seemed to them like sheer confection.

As a large hand suddenly released from the shape
of a fist makes itself all at once gentle, the spread
of his palm reclined, as if to suggest my spine lay
down its love-line. And hadn't I noticed the curtains
were closed, so that no one would know? A desire
replaces me, and my hand cannot pass through its
shadow, the ghost of it grown solid. Someone else
is riding my fever beneath the lavender cover of his
generous dream. How I wish she would wake, undo
her stays, and breathe! Does she not see his pupils
cinch in the light, feel his intent tighten round her
like a corset? *A fainting couch is meant to fall on.*

Just looking at it was lying on it. A palm forever
stunned, pink and spread, fingery and intimate as
anemone, promising always it'd close smoothly
over me, as water will slow its surface, kill brief
ripples into stillness, will never give up the trove
it's acquired, the limbs and tires we willfully cast
to its bottom. *Down there one becomes a never.*
Which means to some the same as forever, your
story so private it will only hand itself over to ears
of water-weed and brack. *When I feel faint, I fear
I may never come back.* A search party wanders
as the ribs in my cage, one by one, begin to snap.

Flood Museum

—Johnstown, Pennsylvania, 2004

Standing above the replica   we hand our eyes down
to roll the curvature of valley   to fall into the embrace
of a glowing lake   its glossy surface pulsating threat
the shape of a handheld mirror   small enough to hold
a face wavering back   slowly liquid in its palm
Tiny lights blink   lights lighting the way water went
by gravity made tremendous   hauling with it a wealth
of debris   the company of iron bridge and tower house
A cataract broken   *it ran out as fast as it could get out*
falling down into the industrial belly of the town igniting
everything   all limbs hauled to burn beneath a bridge
The smell of skin burning hung   each house turned cinder

Who says history is personal   In the museum's gift shop
change-purses, pens, yo-yos   all bear disaster's insignia
so we might dream forever   of a wave's grotesque hand
ride the tangling forth of its froth   wake loud as those
screams simulated on tape loop endless at the tour's end
The town still at its usual best   playing the role of victim
A town with only a flood to its name Without its disaster
why would anyone ever visit   Speaking of the personal
have some history on me   handle gently its particulars
The waylaid lovers serve   a weak broth for this tragedy
My heart's no Penn. thought its economy is equally bleak
I cannot recall how red the red umbrella we stood beneath

Was I so fond of that fantasy   you and me sipping gin
at the lake's bottom   overhearing the faint lapping above
our depths sonic thrusts of a world happening without us
When I begin my composition   I'll set your face to wave
recall for a moment   how the light moves bluely over you
your eyes tight as mollusks   drawn fetal beneath covers
the motel room daylight itching to crawl between curtains
Disaster seems to agree with you, *baby*   I just killed you
You just killed me   At the donut shop I lower an arm
to pull you out the booth   Are we what we wanted to be
or are just you weak   Whoever told you you could love
neglected to mention   you'd have to leave the house

A century since the dam lost its hold yet little's recovered
No one lives here or the few that do seem to for the sake
of recounting a disaster   blame the wealthy for the cries
of children they never knew   they must have the screams
memorized   as a tedious song becomes forever looped
in the mind   Does the guide feel herself an exhibit
recounting a horror   day after day her smile forced
as she doles out yet again   the number of victims
Do not ask what is natural about a disaster of a man-made
lake overtaking man   the dam they built faulty
in the first place   Do not ask which they consider worse
a crime caused by carelessness   a crime born of intention

Vials of muddy water on exhibit   A tear grown so heavy
Some far off brackish thing stinks of an unkempt promise
The gross beast of an ideal languishes   on rank sands
We got this far in and we are landlocked Sea pulsing deep

82

its distant wounds in the ear   I never saw a tear so dirty
or had an eye so full of dirt   *Sir be so good as to tell us*
where you were when it broke   All me falls to the center
of a mattress   sunsets flare then dampen with your lashes
I wouldn't say exactly to the quantity   as I had nothing
to measure it by   how to peer down into the silt of your iris
eyes shut as shells   waters rise well above the flood line
It commenced to rain   a dead boy surfaces his terrible paleness

Robotripping

What gets out:
I would be for you   like fog, those puddles
of mist settling in the valleys   cars steer through
nighttime,   mid-Pennsylvania, staking their slow
headlights on   clouds nestled deep in the pits
between mountains.   When your tongue wanders,

dropping indiscreetly its lexicon, as a drunk lady
ignores the slipping strap   of her negligee,
I would hang myself   on your wall like the
taxidermied head of a bison, watch you   eat pills
from behind its glass eyes.   I pack the sexy
nightgown but do not wear it. Your tongue tries it

on, slips.   And I will expose myself, grass blades
to the lowering blades   of your mouth's lawn
mower,   and I will be brave,   will translate
your haze, would be   your muddle's dedicated
scholar, undo each word   from your mumble
and squeak it clean,   would for you sleep

one week to stay   awake the next, would dump
my jewelry into the river,   cross the suspension
bridge to see you fall out your truck's door, catch
the words   that spill out the pockets I worm
my hands through, looking for the lost room key.
I would be the worm   to your rain soaked side

walk. And would be brave,   translate your late
night mutters, love you best   hungover, fold
your clothes,   place your folded clothes on
the corner chair, scare the clerk out when you've
slept past check-out time.   I would bring you
a glass of water.

Poem That Wears Your Scarf

knows my milky neck as I stand street-cornered,
rivering one last look at you back toward my iris.
Market bouquets jut fierce heads out the collars
of their paper cones. Everywhere signs appall:
Fresh Cut Flowers, the violet blooms heralding
dismay I am moving toward you in this peopled
square. Even at this distance, the two blue disks
set in your head conduct their hypnosis, revolve
like pinwheels, pale twins that spin me epileptic.
My eyes dark as wish-coins tossed to fade slowly
into the murk at a fountain's bottom, your eyes
so light they look lighter than ice, a pale closer
to nothing than any iris I've seen: as the distilled
clarity of a drink looks weak and yet is stronger
than one might think. Your eyes that did me in.

It begins again with you, succulent darling, your
mouth pressing so hard at mine our teeth *clack*.
All kisses should be so onomatopoetic, all love
should be loud enough to scare off the neighbors.
We put the reds of our tongues to bed, tuck them
deep in the jewelry boxes of our mouths. Falling
from out the doorway hinged to a strange man's
house to land on the peculiar glittering of asphalt
at 5 a.m., a new sun so diamond and inexplicable
shuddering up brick walls. The taxi was waiting
around the corner, but we didn't notice the corner.

Why was it taking so long? We never, never sleep
again. Days later, on a train heading south, your
head falls, perches itself like a boulder on the sharp
edge of my shoulder. I sneeze blood into a napkin.

Did you know I liked how our bodies flinched?
Your bed tight with ice covers, never a place for
lovers. Your floors slick and fogged, set as still
and hard as the face of an opaque lake. Branches
outside clacking in wind, everywhere a glittering.
The slow syrup of chilled vodka sliding its arctic
snake down my throat. How nights trembled, seal
entrails wetting snow darkly, just-clubbed, while
disco lights revolved all around us, us emptying
drinks into our mouths as criminals shake stolen
purses out, dump their contents into black sacks.
How even the air there was muzzled. I loved being
locked in the walk-in freezer of your apartment
where you fed me paté and chardonnay, allowed
me to watch you sleep. *I love you*, I told the wall.

Moments before the streets will wrap their scarves
around our necks and I will cast my stare out from
the window set at the cab's back, avenues rivering
opalescent behind us, and we step out, oily rainbows
puddling round our boot-heels, I am walking alone.
I do not know your very pale eyes yet. Can I not
sense my desire, as I move languid beneath sun cast
on the sidewalk, for your brand of decadence? *No.*
I will lie in your bed, watch as you peel an orange.

I will allow my mouth to open, let in your fingers.
I lose my hat, I lose my mittens, I lose my head.
When the blizzard hits, all is white, and you stand
me before a mirror, wind your scarf round my neck.
Now I want to push this story down your throat.
I see you cornered on the street corner. I approach.

Colder, Bitterer

My hair turns white overnight. No, my hair is black
and gloves my head, my hair thick, dark as leather,
my hair meaning ever and ever, even after that ever.

My hair is black, take it back. I like the rumor better
that found you in Greenland, allowed us to suspend
your headlong fall in the frail and opaque wilderness

of our minds, still your body midair moments before
its smash into all that white, let us leave you broken
at a glacier's base, ice-locked, lips thistled with frost.

My hair was black, they're bringing you back. When
I think you dead, my hands run over the hair that caps
my head. A rumor had you lodged so deep and far out

they said you would never be recovered, your body lost
by a glacier in Greenland. Not so distant, not so far out,
no, just as gone yet nearer still: your body discovered in

Canada. Men and pulleys pull you out the snow to cut
you open. What do they think they'll find? Your bag
of skin, its loose sock of flesh smashed, bone-shards?

They will cut you open. Everyone is crying. Everyone
and their flowers. Though I hate your lover since I was
once your lover, I still cannot stand to watch her crying

in this stadium of grief. Our jealousies empty the heavens.
Her shoulders shake beneath the sun. My hair turned white.
They carry you off the mountain. They are cutting you open.

You Cut Open

When I used to not watch television, knowing it was bad for the mind.
When I used to listen to the rain, not knowing it was bad for the mind.
Regarding our mourning: we stood in a stadium. The sky grew harried.
Wherever it was, your body, our minds crawled it like flies, thinking it.

Wherever it was, our minds were combing your skin, licking scratches.
Somewhere someone was doing something with your body. Bad minds
trying to find something bad to find. Death unnatural, your fall suspect.

In the stadium, us each thinking ourselves along your limbs like tongues.
Back with your body, in some lab far outside our minds, their procedure
begun, the scalpel's line drawn clean from chest to sternum, the incision

forming a Y. Tugging the flap of skin above your breast back over your
head, skin I kissed folds over your face, meets your blue lips. They saw
off the ice-caps of ribs, then lift them off your chest like lids. Skin flaps

are dropped back to your sides so their hands can dig out the heart-block,
lungs, ropes of intestine, set them all aside to weigh, slice and later view
through a microscope on slides. They saw your skull a hinge, now cup

to gently lift the brain's delicate jelly, suspend it into a jar's formaldehyde.
They put back your skull's cap, leave you witless, and sew your head shut
with the same thick stitch used to stitch baseballs. Now they drop the lot

of you back into you: heart, intestine, lungs, spleen and liver, all a jumble,
back into the space where once together they hummed inside a living you.
Sun knifes light out from the heart of cloud. I want to bury my hands in

your guts, breathe in the mineral rust of your blood gone bad and dead,
rich plush, bury myself beneath your hide, live beneath its ruby slickness,
to push my own bones into you, knot my fingers in your hair's slack flax.
Salt in rock. Water in rock. They're done with you. My eyes crack open.

Jeewon Jung

The Author

Cate Marvin was born in Washington, D.C. She holds MFA degrees from the Universities of Houston and Iowa and a Ph.D. from the University of Cincinnati. Her first collection of poetry, *World's Tallest Disaster* (Sarabande Books, 2001) won the 2000 Kathryn A. Morton Prize and the 2002 Kate Tufts Discovery Award. It was described by *Publishers Weekly* as a "taut, defiant, confessional collection" and by *Ploughshares* as a "spectacular debut." Along with the poet Michael Dumanis, she co-edited the groundbreaking anthology *Legitimate Dangers: American Poets of the New Century* (Sarabande Books, 2006). She teaches in the low-residency MFA Program in Creative Writing at Lesley University and is an associate professor in English at the College of Staten Island, City University of New York.